debbie tucker green

Theatre includes: *a profoundly affectionate, passionate devotion to someone (– noun), hang, truth and reconciliation, random, stoning mary* (Royal Court); *nut* (National Theatre); *generations* (Young Vic); *trade* (RSC); *born bad* (Hampstead) *dirty butterfly* (Soho).

Film and television includes: *second coming, random.*

Radio includes: *lament, gone, random, handprint, freefall.*

Awards include: Radio Academy Arias Gold Award for *lament*; International Film Festival Rotterdam Big Screen Award for *second coming*; BAFTA for Best Single Drama for *random*; Black International Film Award for Best UK Film for *random*; OBIE Special Citation Award for the New York Soho Rep. production of *born bad*; Olivier Award for Most Promising Newcomer for *born bad*.

Other Titles in this Series

debbie tucker green

hang

NICK HERN BOOKS

London

www.nickhernbooks.co.uk

A Nick Hern Book

hang first published in Great Britain in 2015 as a paperback original by Nick Hern Books Limited, The Glasshouse, 49a Goldhawk Road, London W12 8QP, in association with the Royal Court Theatre

Reprinted with revisions 2018

hang copyright © 2015, 2018 debbie tucker green

debbie tucker green has asserted her right to be identified as the author of this work

Cover image: Marianne Jean-Baptiste/Lovers

Designed and typeset by Nick Hern Books, London .
Printed and bound by CPI Group (UK) Ltd, Croydon, CR0 4YY

A CIP catalogue record for this book is available from the British Library

ISBN 978 1 84842 489 0

hang was first performed at the Royal Court Theatre Upstairs, London, on 11 June 2015, with the following cast:

THREE   Marianne Jean-Baptiste
ONE   Claire Rushbrook
TWO   Shane Zaza

Director	debbie tucker green
Designer	Jon Bausor
Lighting Designer	Tim Mitchell
Composer	Luke Sutherland
Sound Designer	Christopher Shutt
Movement Director	Polly Bennett
Assistant Director	Miranda Cromwell
Casting Director	Amy Ball

Characters

ONE, *female*
TWO, *male or female*
THREE, *female*

Character One and Two are of any race. Character Three is Black, she has a slight, nervous tremble in her hand(s) only.

Time: Nearly now.

Words in brackets are not to be spoken.

Names without dialogue indicate an active silence between those characters.

A forward slash (/) marks an overlapping point in dialogue.

ONE   ...So, we'll be in here –

TWO   just along / this –

ONE   not sure if you've been in here before, but
               they mostly –

TWO   they're very samey –

ONE   very samey, good way of putting it.

TWO   The set-up in each is pretty much the same,
               we go from room to room and even we can
               get –

ONE   (*to* TWO) it shouldn't be locked, should be
               unlocked – it was booked – (*to* THREE) just
               here yep – on the left.

THREE   (In) here?

ONE   In (here), yep. (*to* TWO) Thanks. (*to* THREE)
               Just in (here)...

               They enter the room. It is basic, but clean.
               Strip lights automatically flicker on. A water
               cooler with plastic cups stands in the corner.

               THREE *notices the lights snapping on, no*
               one appears to have flicked a switch.

               Automatic, power-saving... things... Sensors
               – bit Star Trek (I) can't get used to them /
               either.

TWO   Think they think we've lost the ability to flick
               a switch.

ONE   Well, to flick a switch / off.

TWO   Can I get you anything?

ONE   Yes, can we get you anything?

TWO   Would you like a drink of – ?

               THREE *shakes her head*.

               We do have more than the water over / there.

ONE   Tea, coffee – decaf and normal, herbal –

TWO   we're out of herbal

ONE   except herbal, a juice or / something?

TWO   anything really – .

               THREE *shakes her head*.

               Y'sure? Nothing's too –

ONE   it's not a problem and anything we don't have
               we can go out and get –

TWO   I can go out and get.

               THREE *goes to say something, then doesn't*.

               Beat.

               TWO *nods*.

               Okay.

ONE   Ummm –

TWO   (*to* ONE) what would you / like?

ONE   you wouldn't / mind – ?

TWO   Nah I don't / mind.

ONE   If you wouldn't mind sorting me out a tea?

TWO   No problem

ONE   if that's okay, don't wanna take liberties or
               anything but / I –

TWO   it's fine –

ONE   sure?

TWO   Yeh.

ONE	Parched, thanks (I) didn't manage to grab anything before we –
TWO	I'm getting something anyway –
ONE	so it's no (problem)?
TWO	My tea's better'n your effort anyway, what d'you – ?
ONE	Builder's. Strong. No sugar.

TWO *nods, exits the room.*

Really, do say if there's anything at any point you feel you need, it won't be a problem.

ONE *gestures for her to take a seat. She doesn't sit.*

…Is your husband (coming)? I think you said he was – did you say he was on his way?

THREE	
ONE	Are we… should I…? Is he going to…?
THREE	
ONE	I don't want to – I mean it's fine if you want us to, need us to hang on for a while we're happy / to –
THREE	He's not coming.
ONE	…Okay. Right. That's, not a problem.
THREE	
ONE	Was it the – . I mean, if the timing is – if it's the schedule –
THREE	he's at work.
ONE	We could, we can always move the – so it's more convenient, if that's, if that would be more convenient for you, both.

THREE

ONE   Am I... Are we – is... anyone else coming?
           Instead?

THREE

ONE   Is anyone else coming to join you? Today?

THREE

ONE   Did you want someone to (come) did you –
           do you want us to contact someone, someone
           else to come and support you (today)? I think
           it was...

           She checks her file.

           '...Suzette' who came with you before?

THREE

ONE   Although that was a while / ago.

THREE   Suzette's not coming.

ONE   Suzette's not / joining?

THREE   She's not coming.

ONE   Is there any other family member you wanted
            to – may want to...?

THREE

ONE   A friend?

THREE
ONE

ONE   No?

            THREE *watches her.*

            ...Nobody else?

THREE   No.

ONE   We can wait if you want don't feel pressurised
            by the clock at all we can wait as long as you

	– if you want us to – if you want someone to join you – please, take a seat.
THREE	
ONE	Doesn't matter which one, we don't have special – no. Nothing specific about our seating arrangements – no names on them or anything, just seats. Anywhere.

THREE *hesitates*.

Anywhere is fine. Really.

Beat.

THREE *sits*.

D'you want me to take your (coat)?

THREE	
ONE	I can take that if you like we've got a – outside there's a proper coat rack and hangers – we insisted we needed something had a meeting, had to have a meeting – have to have a meeting to get anything, have to have a meeting to get anything done. Got it done though, and so someone took a quick trip to Ikea, so I can –
THREE	no.
ONE	No.

That's fine. It's out there anyway.
That's okay, as long as you're okay.

THREE *clocks her*.

As okay as you can be.
The offer's there if you change your mind,
d'you want some water (it) does cool and hot,
well, supposed to be hot comes out a bit
lukewarm, but the cool stuff is properly
chilled if you'd like a glass of that – I'm sayin

'glass' we've got these horrible plastic things they expect us to drink out of – not very green – although I can, we can easily get a proper glass for the water from out in the (kitchen) you didn't want a drink at all did you?

THREE

ONE   No. Well you know it's (there) whenever you want don't hesitate if you change your (mind), in fact I can – we can sort some proper glasses out just in case anyway. Always gives the feeling of drinking like a five-year-old drinking out of plastic...

Beat.

THREE
ONE

ONE   ...D'you want to phone anyone? D'you want to phone someone, you can use the phones from here if you want or if you want me to contact anyone on your –

THREE   no.

ONE   To, sit with you even, just a bit of –

THREE   no.

ONE   Some people do find it useful just to have another body in the room another someone in the room that isn't me and some people –

THREE   I'm not some people.

ONE   No, of course – I was just – .

THREE   I have been here before.

ONE   Of course.

THREE   I know how this works.

ONE   Well this is slightly – . We haven't – you haven't... Yeah.

THREE

ONE   No.

               Beat.

               …How have you been?

THREE

ONE   It's been a while.

               THREE *watches her.*

               (A) couple of years isn't it, how have you
               been… keeping?

               THREE *says nothing.*

               Stupid question I know, but…

THREE   Yeah.

THREE
ONE

ONE   I know, I – .
               No / I –

THREE   No. You don't know.

ONE   I can only imagine.

THREE   No. You can't.

ONE   …I'm just (saying)… You do look
               surprisingly well considering all – .

THREE   (*dry*) Thank you.

ONE   I'm not trying to be – and it, I know it sounds
               (wrong) but you do look well, considering,
               with all / you've…

               THREE *exhales slowly.*
               TWO *hustles in with two hot drinks.*

TWO   Tea. Builder's, no sugar and… coffee for me –
               (*to* THREE) if you do change your mind or
               want me to pick you up anything just let / me –

ONE	She doesn't want anything.
TWO	Just saying that if she –
ONE	she's fine. Thanks.
TWO	D'you know how long your husband will be?
ONE	He's not –
TWO	we can wait, won't mind / waiting.
ONE	he won't be joining us today.
TWO	Oh. Right. Right.

Beat.

We can wait if you want us to wait if it's an issue with his work or / something.

ONE	He's not –
TWO	or if you wanted someone else / then –
ONE	it's – no. Thanks. We've been over (that)…
TWO	Oh.

ONE *sips their tea, it is disgusting.*

So we're not waiting / for – ?

ONE	Would you – d'you mind popping back out while I remember we do need some glasses, something for the –
TWO	oh, sure yeah –
ONE	*clean* ones, y'know what they can be like, just in case we feel for some –
TWO	yeh, sure, why some can't be left in here I don't (know) I did bring it up, but obviously that'll take another / meeting.
ONE	y'know, if we wanted to take some water or something, or else there's only these –

TWO	nightmare
ONE	yeh these plastic things in here –
TWO	nightmare
ONE	horrible to drink out / of.
TWO	feel like a five-year-old drinking out of one of them
ONE	*exactly*. If you wouldn't mind – I feel like I'm taking / the –
TWO	No no, not at all. I know what you mean, they're nasty, not nice to drink out of at all
ONE	no.

TWO *disappears out of the room again.*

Beat.

…Does your husband know you're here?

THREE

ONE   I mean – I know it's none of my – but I am concerned if you feel you have to shoulder all of / this on your –

THREE   He knows I'm here.

ONE   And he knows what's – where we are in the process of – ?

THREE

ONE   Right.

THREE

ONE   Right.
        And does he have an opinion / on –

THREE   The family does. Know.

Beat.

ONE   Okay.

THREE   Suzette knows. My husband knows. The whole
               family knows. Why I'm here.

               ONE *nods*.

               And I don't need your concern.

ONE   Right.

THREE   Your concern can do exactly – what?

THREE
ONE

THREE   Exactly. And I don't need your compliments.

ONE

THREE   Your compliments can do exactly, what?

               Beat.

ONE   Right.

THREE   Exactly.

ONE   …You discussed with them –

THREE   I've *told* them.

               I've *discussed* with my husband.
               I've *told* my family.
               (*dry*) If that's okay with you?

ONE   I – . Yes. I didn't mean to –

THREE   I think y'did.

ONE   And… Are you in agreement? You and /
               your –

THREE   You're right. It is none of / your –

ONE   It's none of my business I / know.

THREE   Yes.

ONE   Yes. No.

               TWO *bursts back in with a stack of clean
               glasses*.

TWO	There was nothing that matches but then I saw the stash someone had got on that Ikea run hidden at the back like they didn't wanna be found. Anyway perfect for us, washed and clean – I'll just...

TWO *tries to stand the glasses on the water cooler, that doesn't work. Self-consciously* TWO *ends up placing them elsewhere.*

	Sorted.

TWO *notices the spare chair.*

	Do we need – ?
ONE	No.
TWO	Suzette?
ONE	No.
TWO	No, okay.

TWO *removes one of the chairs and stacks it with the others to the side of the room.*

	Just so we... (*to* ONE) Have you – ?
ONE	Yes.
TWO	Okay.
ONE	Yep.
TWO	I wasn't sure if –
ONE	yeh. I made sure first thing.
TWO	Okay / good.

TWO *sits taking a swig of coffee. It is disgusting. Flicks a switch.*

THREE	Is this being recorded?
TWO	This?
ONE	No.

TWO	God no. That (switch), that's air-con.
ONE	We'll be boiling in a minute and freezing the next –
TWO	bit of a nightmare
ONE	have you adjusted / the – ?
TWO	Trying, but it seems to do its own thing.

TWO *adjusts the settings*.

ONE	Technology.
TWO	We've got a remote and the remote is for this, not for any – so no. We wouldn't record –
ONE	not this.
TWO	Not you.
ONE	No.
TWO	You've done nothing wrong you're not a suspect and that would be – y'know, that would cross all sorts of boundaries. I think. No. That – no.
ONE	No audio. No visual. No two-way…

THREE *doesn't understand the term 'two-way'*.

TWO	mirrors, two-way mirrors, / y'know –
ONE	None of that. Just us. In the room. This is about you and about you feeling as comfortable as we can make you feel.
THREE	
TWO	Which probably isn't very comfortable at all. We are aware of that.
THREE	
ONE	We are aware of / that.

THREE	Are you.
TWO	We've been made aware of that.
THREE	Have you.
TWO	A big part of that was pointed out in training –
THREE	was it.
ONE	Well –
THREE	training to teach you that.
TWO	Well –
THREE	train you hard to know that?
TWO	Umm –
THREE	how *do* you train
TWO	errr –
THREE	for this?
ONE	We, uh, well / we –
TWO	Role-play.
ONE	Amongst other – . There's lots of – it's quite an –
TWO	can be quite an intensive / training –
ONE	extensive and intensive training we have to do, after all the, academic stuff, which is a lot. Exams, grades, assessments, pass marks and that. The usual. Then they get us to, role-playing so / we –
TWO	Different scenarios –
ONE	it's meant to try to help / to –
THREE	Who gets to play me?
TWO	…It's not like that, it's not that / specific.
THREE	Who gets to play me? Or do you swap?

THREE
TWO

ONE   It's not like that.

TWO   It's not like that. No.

THREE   And you couldn't make me comfortable by
                the way. You couldn't make me – I lost any…

ONE   Of course.

                ONE *and* TWO *quietly nod*.

THREE   This isn't very 'comfortable'.

ONE   No.

THREE   (*dry*) Just for the record.

TWO   We're not / recording.

THREE   Not comfortable at all.

TWO   (We) can appreciate that.

THREE   No. You can't.

                Beat.

                Would you even tell me if you were filming
                this?

TWO   We're not allowed to film this.

THREE   You film everything else it seems.

TWO   We're not allowed to not tell you we're
                filming this. Which we are not. If we were
                filming this we would have to tell / you.

THREE   Streets, car parks, parks, shops, alleys… all
                on camera.

ONE   That's the –

THREE   all pointless.

ONE   They can sometimes be –

THREE	all pointless.
TWO	That's a matter of / opinion.
THREE	All fucking pointless.
ONE	
TWO	
THREE	Stops nothing. Deters nothing.

Does it?

Did it.

She goes to say something else, but changes her mind.

I'll take that water. Please.

TWO	Yeh, sure –
ONE	no problem, I'll get / it.
TWO	Yeh?
ONE	Yep.
TWO	Fine.
ONE	Did you want the hot –
TWO	that one only does lukewarm really –
ONE	or chilled?
THREE	…Both. Not full.
ONE	…Okay.

TWO *looks briefly confused.*
ONE *fixes two glasses of water from the water cooler, one cold one warm.*
She gestures to TWO.

D'y'mind if you –

TWO	huh?

ONE   The – if you could –

               ONE gestures, TWO *understands and sorts a place for the glasses of water closer to* THREE.

TWO   (Of) course. Yep. Goddit.

               ONE places both glasses down carefully.

ONE   Let me know if that's not – .

               They both watch as THREE *sips some of the chilled, then adds some of the lukewarm water to take the chill off it. She has a noticeable shake in her hands, they see.*

TWO   …How's Tyrell? And Marcia?

               THREE *considers the question.*

THREE   …Y'know.

               TWO *nods.*

TWO
THREE

ONE   They must be, what now? Eleven and –

THREE   ten. And twelve.

               ONE *nods.*

ONE   Getting big. And two of them. My seven-year-old's going on seventeen. Already a nightmare, busy telling me about the world at / seven!

TWO   Wonder who she gets that / from?

ONE   Keep tellin my husband – well, ex-husband now since we last (met) – keep telling him that he needs to clamp down on all / that.

THREE   I miss Marcia's noise.
               I miss my Marcia's chatter.

I miss her foolishness. Her childishness.
Her childhood.

She's missing her noise, her chatter, her
childishness.
Her childhood.
She, wonders where it's gone.

TWO	
THREE	
THREE	Tyrell has gone from…

*ONE and TWO sip from their disgusting
drinks.*

Beat.

	When did you split? *turns it on 'one'*
ONE	This isn't about me, this / is – └ *re-interrogation*
THREE	Why did you split?
ONE	Really, this – . This isn't, you're here for –
THREE	I know why I'm here, don't think I've forgotten.
ONE	No. (Of) course / not.
THREE	I don't think I would forget.
ONE	No.
THREE	I haven't forgotten.
ONE	No.
ONE	
THREE	How long ago did you…?
ONE	…Eighteen months.
THREE	
ONE	And six days.
THREE	Still counting.

ONE	Nope.
THREE	
ONE	
ONE	…The job. Pressures. Hours and all that, usual stuff – really it's just – today is about (you) –
THREE	amicable?
ONE	No.
THREE	(Did) you split from / him?
ONE	No. Listen I'm – y'know, I'm sure my husband – ex-husband would give a different reason and a very different version –
TWO	and today is / about –
ONE	but this isn't about / all that.
TWO	no. It's not about that, *this* is about –
ONE	today is about you
TWO	today is all about / you.
ONE	and we want to focus on you.
THREE	This isn't about me. I think it's all about him. Still. This isn't about me, today. He wants to know. You want to know. You want to know so you can tell him. He wants to know what you know so he will know where he stands. I'm here. So you can know. So you can tell him. So he can find out.

…This isn't about me at all. Is it?

You want to know my decision. |
| ONE | …We're in no hurry, we / know – |

THREE	You want to know my decision.
ONE	We know it's a big decision to make.
THREE	(*dry*) 'You know it's a big decision to / make.'
ONE	We know it's a tricky position to put you / in.
THREE	I've been in a 'trickier' / position.
ONE	And we know it's a decision none of us will really be able to appreciate the scale / of –
THREE	I've been in 'trickier' positions. I've been in 'trickier' positions haven't I?
ONE	
THREE	This isn't that big a decision at all. This isn't that difficult. And what version would your husband say – ex-husband have said, / say?
ONE	What?
THREE	About why you split / up.
ONE	That really doesn't / matter.
THREE	You asked me about my kids.
TWO	I was just –
THREE	you asked me about my husband.
ONE	I just –
THREE	'training'? Cos I'm 'just' askin, back.
THREE ONE	
ONE	I dunno he… …He'd… I mean, I / dunno –
THREE	You cheated?

ONE	It's a pressurised job.
THREE	I can only imagine –
ONE	it's-it's a lot of pressure
THREE	(I) can only imagine
ONE	you end up taking the hours home with / you.
THREE	can only imagine how pressurised it must be. For you.
TWO	D'you want me to hang your coat? It doesn't need to be on your / lap –
THREE	No.
TWO	I can hang your coat on the –
THREE	no
TWO	outside we've got a new –
ONE	no / it's –
TWO	had to get a / new –
ONE	we've been over –
THREE	I know, Ikea
TWO	yes!
ONE	We've been over that and it's fine. The coat's fine.
TWO	…Great. Okay. Just say if you – and you're alright with the air-con? Actually, might be a good idea to keep your coat close, you're ahead of us there. Hot one minute, minus whatever the next.

Beat.
Beat.

THREE	Tyrell has gone from that… open aspect of you, thatchu only have when you're young. Very young.

Before, life batters you into defensiveness,
before life has had its way with you,
before life has scared you – scarred you,
before life has worn you, overwhelmed you
held your head under and kept you, there.

Tyrell has gone from that open-faced, open-
minded, open-hearted little boy we were
filling up with love and laughter and good
spirit and proper knowledge and all the good
stuff you can as much as you can as much as
we could as parents put their way. He's gone
from that little boy to...

Beat.

Three schools on – didju know that? You got
that in your file? Y'gonna have to amend your
file, we're three schools, six classes, four
teaching assistants on now, for both of them,
seeing as you're asking – they aged overnight
– seeing as you're asking – like me and my
husband seein as you're – I know you want
my decision.

ONE   It's absolutely okay if you haven't made a /
           decision.

THREE   I've made a decision.

TWO   'Three schools on'?

THREE   Three.

TWO   (*quietly*) Shit.

THREE   They've... lost the ability to settle, any ability
           to settle – I say, 'lost'.
           To lose is to misplace.
           To misplace is something you'd do yourself.
           Something you'd do yourself wouldn't fuck
           you up so much.
           They can't settle in a school, they can't settle
           in a class, they can't settle in the house, in

a house, in our house, they are *un*-settled, *still* unsettled, have been unsettled – unsettle-able, *un*-settling, we're trying to…

THREE *takes a sip of her water* (*her hand still has its tremble*). *Says nothing else.*

ONE *nods.*

ONE   …I know you've heard it a thousand times and I know it's not helpful – can't help but / I'm (sorry) –

THREE   It's not helpful.

ONE   I really / am –

THREE   It's not helpful.
             And I've not heard it a thousand times before.

ONE   No.

THREE   No.
             People are too embarrassed to say anything.
             To say anything of use.
             To say anything of use any more.
             People say nothing, presume I've stopped waiting for them to say anything. To say anything useful. People presume I'm, over it. Over the worst.
             People have got tired of talking about it, they're all cried out about it.
             Suzette's stopped speaking about it –

ONE   I can only –

THREE   so we've stopped speaking. So I've lost a sister as well.

ONE   I can only / imagine.

THREE   No you can't. You *can't* you couldn't get anywhere near.

ONE   I appreciate that.

THREE *watches her.*
Beat.

TWO   …There's also –

THREE   there's always an 'also' –

ONE   (*to* TWO) not now

TWO   no, I / mean –

ONE   not now.

THREE   What 'not now'?

ONE   Nothing.

THREE   There's 'nothing' not now? What?

               Beat.

ONE   (*quietly*) There's… There's been a… there's also been a –

TWO   development.

ONE   …Development, yes.

TWO   There's been a – and it's nothing about your decision nothing to influence your – and we / can –

ONE   We can wait to inform you of it until after you have said what you want to / say.

THREE   'Development'?

ONE   It's not a great – not a legal –

TWO   nothing court-orientated or legalese or anything like / that.

ONE   and it's not why you're here, nothing to do with what today's meant to be / about.

TWO   But –

THREE   but.

THREE
TWO

THREE	You think I need to know.
TWO	It's something to know
THREE	do *you* think I need to / know?
ONE	We have to let you know.
THREE	Will knowing it help me?
ONE	I'm not sure what would help you.
THREE	You think it will sway me?
ONE	I don't think it – it's not about / whether –
THREE	Do you think it would influence me?
ONE	I don't think you're easily influenced.
THREE	Do you think it will change my mind?
ONE	I don't think your mind is easily changed.
THREE	No.
ONE	No.
	It's not about that.
TWO	Really.
THREE	Right.
	Is your 'development' even relevant then?
TWO	
ONE	
THREE	Do you think it's relevant? To me? For me?
ONE	I… I can't say –
THREE	do *you* think it's relevant?
TWO	I –
THREE	do you?
TWO	…I, it's… one of those things.
THREE	'One of those things.'

TWO	It's just / that –
THREE	When have your 'alsos' and your 'one of those things' and your 'developments' ever helped me? Us?
	Ever eased me.
	Ever eased us.
	Ever made my shit better – *ever* made our shit better. Nothing's better. Everything is worse. Do I get a choice to know what this 'development' is?
ONE	Ummm –
TWO	we – / err –
THREE	Or is your 'development' being forced on me?
TWO	We don't want to seem not transparent in / our –
THREE	'Transparent'?
ONE	We think it's best you have all information available as we –
TWO	as discussed in the early stages of this / case.
ONE	and as you requested.
THREE	
ONE	We're just trying to –
THREE	a 'transparent development'
ONE	it's something that's come up and we're just, y'know –
THREE	'transparently' putting it my way –
ONE	yes.
THREE	Whether I want to know or not.
TWO	I know it must feel like we –

ONE	(*to* TWO) no you don't (know) you do not know.
TWO	Er, no, I / don't.
THREE	(*dry*) Right.
ONE	You can absolutely choose to proceed to go no further with / it.
THREE	(*dry*) Right
ONE	no further with the development –
THREE	is this your way of making me increasingly 'comfortable'? You and your 'transparency' policy that you've role-played out I presume – you and your 'development' that you casually fuckin drop – him and his wanting to fuckin / know –
TWO	We absolutely respect that transparency can be / difficult.
THREE	you have no absolutes here. *None*. Unsay what you've just said. I want to un-know what you just told me about your, 'development'. Unsay it.

Unsay it.

TWO *looks at* ONE *unsure.*

Is how I'd like to proceed.

ONE	While I know that I don't exactly 'know', I can only appreciate how hard it must continually be / to –
THREE	Oh, fuckin / don't.
TWO	I think we're getting crossed wires / here.
THREE	Just fuckin don't / yeah?
TWO	I think we're miscommunicating this a bit –

ONE   slightly

THREE   (*quietly*) fuck.

TWO   We don't want you to feel that / we –

THREE   Because it seems to me that, everytime there
                is a 'development' that '*development*' affects
                my family.
                Your developments
                affect my Marcia
                affect my Tyrell
                affect my husband
                affect my marriage.

                Your developments affect my sleep
                how I sleep
                that I don't sleep. Can't sleep. Still.
                It affects their schooling
                affects their schools
                their grades
                their prospects
                their future.
                Fucked their future.
                Affects where we live
                fucked where we lived.

                Affects my health
                my husband's health
                my kids' health – mental and physical.
                Affects their concentration
                affects my work
                my housework
                my day to day
                my laundry – washing piss-stained sheets
                every day,
                changing beds – *every day*
                reassuring them *every day* and knowing it's
                not workin.
                All of us knowin it's not working.

Everybody double and triple checkin locks,
window locks, door locks, Chubb locks, dead
locks, metal grills.
That's our household. You have no fuckin idea
how shit *how shit*... that feels. *This* feels.

We look at each other different.
We talk to each other different.
We move around each other carefully we're
careful with each other, cautious with each
other my son is scared of his shadow and my
daughter pisses in her pants – how's that for
a fuckin 'development'?

And if you tell me 'you know' or-or 'you can
appreciate that' I swear to God I'm fuckin
likely / to –

TWO	I can see how upsetting this / is –
THREE	this isn't me upset. Trust me. *Trust me*. This ent *that*.

THREE *struggles to calm her breathing.*

ONE	...We've been put in this position –
TWO	we didn't see this coming I'm sorry that I – that / we –
THREE	And didju?
ONE	What?
THREE	*Didju?*
ONE	
THREE	Cheat on him? Your husband – ex-husband.
TWO	...We have this situation – and –
THREE	*didju?* Didju find time amongst your 'long hours' amongst all the, 'pressures' of the case, 'pressures' of the job...?

ONE THREE	
THREE	Find time to have a little fling-ting with someone / else?
ONE	As I said –
THREE	somebody else's somebody else? Didju?
ONE	Today is all about / you.
THREE	I think you did. I think you did.
ONE THREE	
TWO	I didn't mean for this to – we didn't mean for this to…
THREE	
TWO	And we're absolutely behind you one hundred per cent, if that will make it / less –
THREE	Can / you –
TWO	somehow make it a fraction / less –
THREE	will / you –
TWO	of course if / you –
THREE	can you / please –
TWO	y'know if you need / to –
THREE	can you please *stop* fucking talking.

Beat.

…God.

Beat.
Beat.
THREE *takes a sip of the tepid water.*
ONE *and* TWO *toy with their disgusting drinks.*

ONE	(*quietly*)…I'm not proud, not proud of it. He knows that.
TWO	(*quietly to* ONE) D'you want me to –
ONE	(*quietly to* TWO) nah. You're alright.
	Beat.
THREE	I don't… give a shit about your, 'development' y'know / that.
ONE	Okay. That's understood. That's okay. (*to* TWO) We don't have to move forward on that / front.
TWO	(*to* ONE) I thought we –
	ONE *and* TWO *talk quietly and quickly between themselves.*
ONE	(*to* TWO) we'll just go back and –
TWO	but they think we're – they're going on the presumption / we're –
ONE	we'll have to go back and tell them no, we'll schedule a meeting and I'll go back and tell them no – it's / perfectly –
TWO	I'm not laying it at your door –
ONE	it's perfectly legit and in fact they should have an option for this, should have had an option for / this.
TWO	I agree –
ONE	so it isn't / any –
TWO	I agree – I do, I / agree.
ONE	and it's not anything that needs to get –
TWO	no. I agree
ONE	and could and *should* prompt a bigger discussion than it / has.

TWO	a larger discussion is outstanding and they know / it.
ONE	They do and they keep –
TWO	I know, they do – I / agree.
ONE	so, y'know –
TWO	yeah. / Exactly.
ONE	The letter doesn't need / to –
TWO	It doesn't –
ONE	it won't need / to –
THREE	A letter?
ONE TWO	
THREE	A 'letter'?
ONE	I think…
TWO	'Development'.
THREE	From who?

She watches them.

From, who?

She watches them.

To who?

ONE TWO	
THREE	…Fuck me, the fuckin / front.
ONE	He wanted to –
THREE	what he wants right?
ONE	He wanted to put something down / on –
THREE	What *he* wants?

TWO	There was no prompting –
THREE	what he wants / *right*?
TWO	this wasn't a programme of any sort or / anything.
THREE	*Felt* like it did / he?
ONE	It wasn't anything to do / with –
THREE	Part of his 'rehabilitation' is / it?
TWO	No this isn't –
ONE	we didn't see this / coming.
THREE	He's decided he's got something to say?

She watches them.

A '*development*'?!

ONE	We don't have to – we really don't have / to –
TWO	You *don't* have / to –
THREE	I *know* I don't have to I *know* I don't have to *anything*. You don't stop fuckin tellin me.

Any other surprises you got to give? Any other 'developments'?

ONE

TWO

TWO	I know this is –
THREE	what do *you know*? *What-the-fuck-do-you-know?* Y'look about twelve years old and sit in front of me and nod your head and drink your drink and tell me 'you know' – you know *nothing* and you (*to* ONE) – you who got a bit of the nine-to-five pressure, just enough to start playing away, what-the-fuck do you know about living with any of this?

	And I'm glad – *glad* amongst all your 'long hours' and untold 'pressure' you somehow managed to find the time to fuck-about cos me and my husband have stopped fucking ever since. What do you exactly (*know*)? About, you *fuckin* 'know'.
TWO	I'm sorry. I –
THREE	you wouldn't know where sorry starts or would you role-play that to find out?
ONE	It's not like that.
TWO	It's not like / that.
THREE	How would you role-play explaining to *your* kids? How would you do your version a that? Who played my Tyrell and who was my Marcia?
ONE	It's not – we don't, we didn't / do – .
THREE	You wouldn't have the course for it. You wouldn't have the paperwork for it. You wouldn't have enough mugs of Ikea tea for it. You wouldn't have the words, the stomach, the imagination for it.
THREE ONE	
THREE	And I dunno what you would suggest you would have done with a seven-year-old that couldn't stop shaking. For hours. And a nine-year-old that was staring into a space that isn't there. For hours. A seven-year-old whose shake couldn't be eased with a squeeze, who saw me shaking more than she was as much I was trying to hold my shit together. For those hours. And wasn't.

A seven-year-old who flinched at my shit
touch of comfort knowing that it won't. That
it couldn't, do nuthin. That it can't. That it
doesn't do nuthin. Still doesn't do anything –
years later. To comfort. Her.

And my, open-faced, open-hearted nine-year-
old son snapped shut, shut down in seconds
after seeing…
And I looked to see what my beautiful boy
was seeing as he stood staring, into nothing.
Some middle distance somewhere I couldn't
access – still can't.
And, he was the screaming one – he was the,
his pitch so high it tore through-your-skull-one.
He was the screaming one that didn't stop for
three hours straight. Staring into nothing and
screaming straight. He was the one whose
scream only stopped when his voice ran out.
That had run, even when we couldn't.
And we couldn't.

And he's hollow now.
His voice is hollow. His eyes are hollow.
His smile, if you get one after all this time,
is hollow. He goes through the family
motions, hollow.
Like the rest of us.

And I dunno what *you* would say to the
shivering seven-year-old you only noticed
hadn't said anything after the screaming
nine-year-old's voice had run dry.
Marcia uttered nuthin. *Nothing*. For four days
after that night.

The years me and my husband had of filling
them up with the good stuff fucked in less than
five minutes. Or was it ten. Or fifteen. Or was
it the whole evening? I don't even fuckin…

You tell me what to do then.
When my kisses drown in their tears.

When they flinch from my own touch.
When they flinch from any touch.
You tell me what to do then.
When they are inconsolable.
When it is unexplainable.
When I am lost for words.
When speaking softly scares them
when my silence hurts them
when my words are wrong
when a raised voice has outrageous
repercussions,
when they've seen their dad damaged, their
mother motionless, our marriage disfigured,
our family fucked.

When I know, and *they* know I do not have the
ability – the capability left in me to help them
whatsoever cos they can see I can hardly help
myself – you tell me what to do then, what to
say to them then. Please. You tell me that. Cos
that's a development.

ONE

TWO

THREE   They're on meds to stop them shaking,
             meds to force them to a sleep,
             meds to stop them dreaming,
             meds to wake them up,
             meds to keep them awake,
             meds to calm them down…
             They're medicated day by day. Just to get
             them through one.

             ONE *and* TWO *watch her.*

             And I say what to my husband when neither
             of us have the words left to say anything to
             each other?

             ONE *and* TWO *say nothing.*

Where's that in your manual? In your
role-play? In your meeting about a meeting
about how to make me feel 'comfortable' –
ask about my kids again I fuckin dare you.

ONE *goes to say something, doesn't.*
Beat.
Beat.
ONE *subtly gestures to* TWO *who makes a*
silent excuse and leaves the room.

…When did he write it?

ONE	
THREE	Don't make me ask you / again.
ONE	Four days.
THREE	
ONE	We received it, four days / ago.
THREE	I asked when he wrote it.
ONE	We only received it four days ago if we'd got it any earlier we'd have informed / you.
THREE	I asked you, when he wrote it.
ONE	…It's, er, it's-it's dated around six weeks ago I believe.
THREE	Believe or know.
ONE	Know.

THREE *takes it in.*

(It) can take a while to work through the
system before it gets to us. If we'd known
earlier we could / have –

THREE	Have you read it?
ONE	…It's been read.
THREE	Have *you* read it?

ONE	It's been / read.
THREE	Are you trying your hardest to / fuckin –
ONE	I'm not at liberty to say if I've read it or / not.
THREE	Have you *read* it?
ONE	
THREE	Have you read it?
THREE ONE	

A silent battle of wills.

ONE	…It's on file.
THREE	(*quietly*) It's on file. 'It's on file.'

I walk the streets of a neighbourhood I live in now that I don't know. Got lost last week ended up somewhere else. Somewhere else but still with the same me in it. It would be funny if it was funny.

ONE *nods.*

(Is that) a nod of agreement?
A nod of acknowledgement?
A nod that it's 'fine' –

ONE	a nod of sympathy.
THREE	(*quietly*) Sympathy. (*quietly*) Fuck your sympathy and keep it with your 'sorries' how many more letters are there?
ONE	Just this one.

TWO *re-enters the room.*

THREE	(*to* TWO) She was saying you found the contents of the letter repulsive.
TWO	There's nothing abusive within it which would have stopped us considering / it for –

THREE	So you've read it.
ONE	(*quietly*) Shit.
THREE	She's told me most of it but I just wondered what you…?
	TWO *is confused*.
TWO	I –
ONE	it doesn't matter.
TWO	Have I – ?
ONE	Yeh.
TWO	Shit.
ONE	Yeh.
TWO	Sorry.
ONE	
TWO	Shit.
THREE	What did you, make of it? The contents of it that 'have nothing abusive within it which'… what?
TWO	I shouldn't have (said) we're not allowed / to –
ONE	If you want to know, it's here for you to read yourself –
THREE	but you've read it
TWO	I'm not –
THREE	'allowed to' but you've let some shit slip already so you can give me the… gist.
TWO THREE	
THREE	Can't you.
TWO	

THREE	Or are you wilfully withholding... wow. After all this it's like I gotta beg? No.
ONE	We've – there's / protocol.
THREE	I will not / beg.
ONE	There's the protocol.
THREE	Fuck protocol.
TWO	We can't. We can't / just –
THREE	Protocol didn't happen in my house to me and mine he didn't give a *fuck* about protocol, and you sit there and you shroud his-his, *shit*, in your rules and regs – when he-when he, what. *What?* And I begged him back then, but I'm not fuckin begging you now – I beg nobody. Nothing. Never. No. / Not again.
ONE	I think it would be good – and we can make the phone call if necessary, for you to have someone else here with you. I do. I / do.
TWO	I do.
ONE	This isn't easy, I – we knew it wouldn't be easy but I think we all underestimated how hard this would be. Could / be.
THREE	D'you / think –
ONE	I think –
THREE	d'you think I can't take it?
ONE	I think this is unfair.
THREE	You think I can't take / it.
ONE	I think this is unfair. On you.
THREE	This is the easy bit. And I will and I am taking it, personally.

THREE
ONE
THREE
TWO

THREE   …Where is it?

               Beat.

TWO   I have it.

THREE

TWO   Here.

               TWO *gestures to the file.*
               THREE *watches the file.*

THREE

THREE   …Can I see it?

TWO   Sure.

               TWO *pulls the enveloped letter out and holds*
               it out to THREE.
               THREE's *eyes stay firmly on the envelope.*
               TWO *places it carefully down.*
               Beat.

THREE   (*quietly*) My decision is made. You do know
               that.

ONE   We know that.

TWO   We respect that / and –

THREE   You know that.

TWO   And this isn't in any way meant to, do
               anything to influence your – we didn't see
               this coming.

THREE

ONE   Look… This feels like we're cocking this up
               every which way, we, sincerely want to-to, try
               and make this as painless – I know my

fucking words are all wrong and it's not coming out right but we are trying to, we really don't want you to feel any more than you – any worse than you / already –

TWO   Absolutely I agree and when we read the letter five weeks ago maybe we should have warned you or-or done something else so that you don't feel quite / so...

ONE   (*quietly*) Fuck.

THREE   'Five weeks ago.'

TWO *nods*.

He wrote it five weeks / ago.

TWO   We *read* it five weeks ago, he wrote it (*to* ONE) when exactly did he write it? A couple of months before / then?

ONE   Fuck.

THREE   ...Yeah.

They wait in an awkward silence.
Distant sounds from an office beyond can be heard including some short bursts of inappropriate laughter.
TWO *isn't sure what the problem is.*

Still they wait.

ONE   D'you mind if we – ?

THREE

TWO   What?

ONE   D'you mind if we – we'll just –

TWO   what?

ONE   Just for two minutes.

THREE

ONE   (*to* TWO) Shall we – ?

TWO	Huh?
	ONE *is up, gestures to confused* TWO.
ONE	(We) won't be long.
THREE	

ONE *gestures again for* TWO *to get up.*
They both exit the room.
THREE *is left alone.*

Beat.
She exhales slowly. She is tired.
Beat.
Her eyes scan the room and drift over to the
envelope, she watches it intently.
Noises from the office beyond bleed into the
room, ignored.
She sips from her water, drains the glass. Her
hands still have their tremble.
Beat.
She crosses to the water cooler and with a
fresh glass draws a chilled glass of the clear
water. Her hands still have their tremble.
Beat.
She re-sits.
She sips from her fresh glass of water, glass
visibly shaking.
Beat.

ONE *and* TWO *re-enter with fresh hot drinks.*
TWO *looking like s/he has taken a bit of a*
bollocking.

ONE	(I'm) sorry for that for the short absence, we didn't mean to – are you sure we can't get you anything? Can we get you something?
THREE	No.
ONE	Someone's just been out so we're freshly stocked, there's a load of herbal options now

as well, camomile, mint, ginger… umm,
camomile – mint – ginger and… and some,
umm, fruity thing. Meant to be / nice.

THREE   How long does it take?

ONE   'Scuse me?

THREE   …How long does it take. To work?

ONE   I don't quite – what?

TWO   (It) depends on which method.

ONE   What?

TWO   …Depends on which method.

THREE   …How long does each 'method' take to work?

            Beat.

TWO   …Each have their own protocols.

THREE   How long does each 'protocol' take to / work?

ONE   You should have been sent some – did you
            not get sent the leaflets, the literature? You
            should have received some information /
            regarding –

TWO   I can get some now we always keep a stock
            here just in case – there's loads left over if
            that would be / useful.

THREE   How long does it take?

ONE   Well… this is gonna sound – but I've gotta
            say it, y'know… and you're not gonna like it
            but… We're not allowed to influence your
            decision in any way –

THREE   you're not influencing my / decision.

ONE   we're not allowed to influence your decision in
            what we say – how we say what we say in any
            way we say it. Which is why the literature –

THREE	leaflets
ONE	were sent. Has been sent, have been sent. Haven't they?
TWO	Yes.
ONE	Yes. They're important, that aspect is important as they are an independent –
THREE	somebody wrote them.
ONE	Yes, but
THREE	somebody wrote them their way.
TWO	Yes, but –
THREE	and I somehow managed, after reading them, to make up my own mind.
ONE	But this / is –
THREE	I've made my decision.
ONE	It's got to be independent.
THREE	It was independent.
ONE	It's got to be *seen* to be an independent / decision.
THREE	I've made my decision.
TWO	We don't know that.

They eyeball.

THREE   (*dry*) Want me to write it down?
(*dry*) Want me to mime it for you?

Beat.

You couldn't influence me.
You couldn't get nowhere near being influential. Nowhere near.
How long does it take?

ONE	There's the option, there is an option for independent advice free independent advice, if you want that, if you need that.
THREE	
ONE	We can access that – that's supplied by – it's from outside the department and staffed by people who are... not us.
THREE	
ONE	It's a sort of light-touch counselling service –
THREE	(*dry*) you think I need that?
ONE	That's not for us to / say.
TWO	They are housed within the same building so you wouldn't have to travel / too –
ONE	There's a free-phone number and an internal phone in the office for this purpose.
THREE	
ONE	It's a decision that can be a lot to live with that's / all.
THREE	I think I've learnt to live with a lot. Learnt to live with loads, me.
	Beat.
	Beat.
ONE	
ONE	
ONE	... (*quietly to* TWO) Do you know the stats?
TWO	
ONE	(*quietly*) Do you have the stats to / hand?
TWO	(*quietly to* ONE) I know the stats.
ONE	(*to* TWO) Accurately?

TWO	(*to* ONE) Accurately, but –
ONE	you're sure?
TWO	Just off the back of a health-and-safety (course), only interesting thing about the two days was the latest in on the / stats.
ONE	(And) d'you feel –
TWO	I don't –
ONE	d'you feel…?
TWO	'Comfortable'?
ONE	Confident. Confident to –
TWO	am I allowed to – ?
ONE	Confident enough to confidently tell her, accurately –
TWO	but I'm not allowed / to –
ONE	I'm allowing you to.
TWO	You can't allow me to though.
TWO ONE	
ONE	You, don't feel comfortable –
TWO	I don't know what / you're –
ONE	that's fine if you don't feel comfortable / to –
TWO	I just don't want – I mean. I'm not, not wanting to be –
ONE	it's fine –
TWO	it's not
ONE	it's fine it's / fine.
TWO	and I'm not trying to-to, y'know be –
ONE	no no I know you're not.

TWO	Shit.
ONE	I know. And I wouldn't ask you to do something I wouldn't do, I won't. I'm putting you in an unfair / position.
TWO	Shit.
	Beat.
ONE	What I will ask you to do though, is to step out.
TWO	?
ONE	To just – for a moment – a tea break, herbal tea break or somethin, so I don't compromise you in any way if I do anything, say anything, I shouldn't.
TWO	…I think you've just compromised me.
ONE	That's not my intention.
TWO	…This is making me feel like I'm the –
ONE	no, it shouldn't. And you're not. You're not comfortable and you feel compromised and that's unfair –
TWO	but now I'm feeling obstructive
ONE	you're not that. Not that either. You're following the rules. You're doing it by the book. You're doin it right.
TWO	I know the stats.
ONE	I can find out the stats.
TWO	(I) just want to know I'm… covered, if… If, when the shit hits the fan that I've still got a – / y'know?
ONE	I can find out the stats.
TWO	That's all it is, a bit – a little / bit –

ONE	I can do the stats
TWO	but I know them. I *know* them.
ONE	I can do the stats without you.
TWO	You're in the shit more than me.
	THREE *clears her throat.* *She takes a sip of water. They watch the shake* *in her hands.* *Beat.* *Beat.*
ONE	Can we really not get you anything?
THREE	
TWO	…Do you have any preference where you want me to (start)…?
THREE	
TWO	If I start with… if you want me to start / with –
ONE	Are you okay to – ?
TWO	No.
THREE	Injection.
TWO	…Lethal… lethal injection or, Passive Insertion as we like to call it, where d'you want me to –
THREE	how long does it take?
TWO	Do you mean from when they start to walk to – or when they're strapped down to – or just the (mechanics) of it?
THREE	
TWO	From the walk down to them flatlining and a-a satisfied team – a team that are medically satisfied that the client is clinically (dead), we like to leave a thirty-minute window at most. At most.

THREE   'Client'.

TWO   Everyone knows why everyone's there and
the chaplain's already been – even for the
non-believers, who often, suddenly believe
and – yeh, client.

And the, meal's been had – last meal's been
had a memory of some other happier time
although that's where the biggest
consternation usually happens as it will never
taste as good as they remember and it is not
cooked by their mother or how their mother
would cook it, or whatever false memory they
have, so it's not the – never the – however
they (remember). Anyway.
Amazing how many people go out on a
Mackey D's and the err, shower's been taken
and... the last feel of fresh water on skin – no
lotions allowed don't need the skin slippery,
for obvious reasons. And the fresh clothes
approved – a civilian selection instead of the
standard correction issue they've been in for
years. But they're not going out looking like
they just stepped out of a magazine though,
no. Nothing elaborate about how they look,
no. They usually haven't got a clue they've
been inside so long.

And the last conversation with loved ones – if
they have any left, if they have any left that's
still speaking to them, that's already taken
place, so we then get to... with that all done
and dusted we get to-to practicalities. The
practicalities of it.

This is the thirty minutes I mentioned.
They're waiting in the, holding room, with
their spiritual adviser of choice and then
we – . We don't allow our clients –

THREE   'clients'

TWO	prisoners – to walk to the place of execution, for their own sake as much as for ours. It can get unpredictable they can get unpredictable, even though it's only down a few corridors / it –
THREE	How long?
TWO	…Strapping them down to the – so we can wheel them through only takes minutes – if they don't struggle, most don't by this / point.
THREE	How long does it take?

TWO *is slightly thrown.*

ONE	The actual… how long?
TWO	…We're old-skool and do the three-injection protocol. It's safe it's practical –
ONE	it's preferred, right?
TWO	By all. Five restraints – leather, quadruple stitched, fleece-lined for comfort – we're proud of that, legs, arms, waist. Head free to move. Two IVs – one is back-up, one in each arm. IV's through to an adjacent room. One anonymous expert execution team, one warden giving the silent signal, a hush is called for – out of respect – and the saline starts to flow. First protocol is the, pentobarbital – I don't want to blind you with –
THREE	you're not
TWO	that 'knocks them out' – technical term not, sorry – comatose, y'know – well, *technically* not a coma I don't think but I'm not / a –
ONE	I think we get / it.
TWO	second protocol is pancuronium bromide – just say if I'm –

THREE	you're not.
TWO	Right, which paralyses the entire muscle system and stops them breathing, stops them breathing cos the muscles are paralysed –
ONE	got / that.
TWO	but bearing in mind, protocol one has pretty much knocked them out anyway –
ONE	you said.
TWO	Protocol three then, is the potassium chloride, which stops the heart which has been monitored constantly and closely –
THREE	by the 'anonymous expert execution team'.
TWO	By the, expert team. Yes. So. …Minutes really. And if anything doesn't go (right) there is the back-up of the second IV. A lot of clients if they had the choice, would choose this as their preferred method.
THREE	
TWO	I've heard.
THREE	Minutes.
TWO	Minutes.
THREE	
THREE	Gas.
TWO	Trickier. Err, do-able. Expiry by Inhalation to give it its full (title). Obviously everything becomes very – y'know, don't muck about with gas and it can be harder to get a team – the expertise of a team together and the facilities are, have to be – no mucking about a hundred per cent sealed. Not so many places have the necessary standard of equipment,

	health and safety go mad on standards, but enough places still do do it, might be a slightly longer journey to – if you were going to, wanted to –
ONE	that's no longer allowed.
TWO	They don't let / you – ?
ONE	Not any more. Recorded. Can show a recording. But not be there, live. As it were. You can't be there and watch. They can stream it though, with a two-minute delay.
THREE	
TWO	But, gas, do-able, absolutely do-able.
THREE	…Quick?
TWO	I mean. I suppose some could say in some ways it's a simpler –
ONE	how long?
TWO	So, with gas… Y'know, the client goes through the same preparatory protocols I mentioned with Passive Insertion – the injection, so they've seen who they need to see and all that, we don't though, let them wear any old thing for this process. Very straightforward, client in the sealed chamber, strapped to a chair – they're not going to be walking around and just, passing out, y'know – no. Strapped to a chair – experts outside, pulls a (*gestures 'lever'*) dropping potassium cyanide pellets into a-a I dunno vat of…
ONE	sulphuric acid
TWO	that yep. That then forms the cyanide gas that is so (lethal), and does, and does… y'know. The job.
THREE	

TWO	Ummm, again. Minutes. Unless something goes – but, we – they are experts. Not the same team that does the – funnily enough everyone specialises in their own / field.
THREE	How long?
TWO	…Ten minutes would be a disaster and someone would probably get sacked, so y'know, quick. Very / quick.
THREE	Firing squad.
ONE	We don't really do 'firing squads' any more
TWO	no
ONE	no.
TWO	It's more, er…
ONE	More two sharpshooters than a squad system. That-that's quite an old-fashioned way of thinking about it, 'firing squad'.
TWO	Ballistic Expiry. To give it its full / title.
ONE	The firearms used have got better, the people using the firearms are trained better. Less are needed for the same effect. One firearms officer has blanks loaded and one doesn't, simple. Both go away with a clear conscience and their absolute priority is to be accurate with their shot. Regardless. There is a phrase used in training that – I'm paraphrasing, is um – goes along the (lines) something like, 'Imagine this was your dying dog that you were putting out of its misery. You'd aim straight.' Something like that.

TWO *nods in agreement.*

TWO	The client is also strapped to a chair –

ONE	yeh y'know it's not, they're / not –
TWO	they're not running round the place like it's-it's target practice or / something.
ONE	a sitting target, a silent signal – all done in silence out of respect, again, that's a protocol in itself. The heart aimed at and y'know it's over as quick as it takes a bullet to – although they are asked to shoot twice. Just in case. And there's a standby if something fluky happens. And the standby will put one between the eyes at close range if needed. If necessary. Which it usually isn't.
TWO	Quick.
THREE	Beheading.
TWO	Messy.
ONE	Yeah.
TWO	Err, I guess, y'know quick. Led to, kneel down, head – yeah.
ONE	Messy.
TWO	Yep. 'Beheading' is actually, it is actually its full technical / title.
ONE	That one's a staffing issue, not a lot of people can get that right. And it needs to be got right. Technique. A real technique. One chance one time to get that correct, no back-up system.
TWO	Well, to have another hack at it would be the back-up and that is no back-up at / all.
ONE	So that does depend on qualified staff and their availability. And retainability. Retention rates are shit in that department – excuse my language.
THREE	Electric / Chair.

TWO	We don't do that.
ONE	Electric Chair. We don't do / that.
TWO	At present that service has been withdrawn –
ONE	a temporary measure –
TWO	(*to* ONE) yeah, that's been 'temporary' for a while.
ONE	(*to* TWO) Meant to come back online but hasn't / yet.
TWO	(*to* ONE) Have you heard when – ?
ONE	(*to* TWO) Haven't heard a thing they're meant to be having a / meeting.
THREE	Hanging. Hanging.
TWO	More technical than you think. More technical than most people / think.
ONE	A lot of maths goes into that –
TWO	a *lot*.
ONE	Length of rope, weight of client, height of drop, it's-it's – it's a technical one, it really / is.
TWO	Rope too short –
ONE	end up strangled, slowly.
TWO	Too long –
ONE	too much pace on the falling body, too much pressure on the rope not just snapping the neck like it's s'posed to... actual decapitation. Not good.
TWO	Not good.
ONE	No one wants to see / that.
TWO	No one wants to clean up after that. Cleaners. Unions go mad.

ONE	A lot of prep goes into that, a lot. 'Slike a bloody maths O level.
TWO	'Rope Option'.
ONE	'Rope / Option'?
TWO	'Rope Option'. People still just call it hanging though. Impossible to / rebrand.
THREE	I heard the bowels let go after a body's been hung.

Beat.

That the body shits itself. By itself.

ONE	…Can do. Yeh, yep.
THREE	That it… that the body twitches. Still twitches. Even after it's / been –
ONE	Can do. Yes.
TWO	Nervous system and all that, although that can be a bit unnerving – no pun intended. The body-the body is quite amazing at times and… yeah.
THREE	That the eyes and the tongue try to leave the head.
TWO	There can be some… Not pleasant. But. An aspect. Yeh.
THREE	
ONE	These should of all been covered – not in as much detail, but – and I think the Electric Chair section was just inked out instead of edited out which aint great / but – .
THREE	I want him hung.

Beat.

I want him hung.
…That's my decision.

Beat.

That was my decision.

Beat.

And I was never good at maths. Never any
good at maths.
And I hope whoever hangs him is as shit at
maths as I was.
That was my decision when I walked into the
room.
And that is my decision, now.

ONE   …Okay.
           Okay.

           Beat.

           You're sure – ?

THREE   I'm sure.

ONE   You're sure.

THREE   I walked in sure. I'm three and a half years /
           sure.

TWO   Revenge isn't the best motivation to make /
           a –

THREE   This isn't revenge.

TWO   Revenge can lead / to –

THREE   This isn't revenge nowhere near.

ONE   …Is your husband in agreement?

THREE   My husband doesn't have to be in agreement.
           I read the small print.

ONE   I have to ask.

THREE   No you don't.
           I read the small print.

ONE

THREE   My husband wishes worse things on himself,
           than he could ever wish on him.

ONE

TWO   I can get the paperwork, should I get the / paperwork?

ONE   There's a small element of paperwork, we just have to put down what you say, ask you to write down your decision and sign against it.

TWO   A few copies.

ONE   Three, isn't / it?

TWO   Four. And then we scan one / in.

ONE   Yeah yeah.

TWO   We date it as well as there is a cool-down period of fourteen days if you should change your mind...

THREE

TWO   We know this decision can be a lot to live with.

THREE   I can live with it.

ONE   Saying something here then going home / and –

THREE   I can live with it.

TWO   ...I'll get the paperwork then. And the stamp.

        TWO *exits*.

ONE
THREE

        ONE *can't hold her gaze*.

THREE   What does it say in the letter?

ONE

THREE   What does it say in the / letter?

ONE   You know we can't – . The letter is there for you to read. With all due respect.

THREE	'Four days'. 'Five weeks'. Written 'a couple months' earlier. Really. Very fuckin 'respectful'.
ONE	
THREE	
ONE	That. Shouldn't have happened.
THREE	That's, not an apology.
ONE	It's – . That's…
THREE	
ONE	
THREE	What does it say in the letter? What does he say in the letter?
ONE	
THREE	…How long is it? How long is it?
ONE	
THREE	Is it pages? Is it / pages?
ONE	It's not long.
THREE	How many pages?
ONE	It's not long.
THREE	'Not long'.
ONE	Couldn't be long enough.
THREE	…Did he write it or have it written?
ONE	
THREE	Did he write it or have it / written?
ONE	He wrote it.
	Beat.
THREE	Wrote it or typed it?

ONE

THREE   Handwritten or computer come / *on*.

ONE   Handwritten. Handwritten.

THREE
ONE

THREE   How does he start?

                 Do I get a 'Dear'…?
                 A 'Hi'…
                 A 'Hello'…? Does he call me by my married
                 name? First name? He asked for that… Does
                 he even remember my name?

ONE

THREE   Blue ink or black ink?

ONE   We've already told you the procedural
                 protocols which we shouldn't have.

                 I'm not reading it.

THREE   You know what's in it.

ONE   I'm not reading it.

THREE   You know what's in / it.

ONE   I'm-I'm happy to open / it –

THREE   You know what he wrote in / it.

ONE   due to your condition –

THREE   this isn't a condition this is caused this is
                 caused. This was caused.

THREE
ONE

ONE   I'm not going to read it for you.

                 TWO *hustles back into the room with the
                 paperwork*.

                 Sorry, but I'm, not.

TWO *clocks the atmosphere.*

TWO Two pens – just in case – (*to* ONE) IT have got loads *weirdly*, seeing as they don't write down anything. (*to* THREE) Both black for scanning purposes if you could date them in your own hand too, although we do have a stamp just to confirm and make it more than obvious to those who will look at this afterwards when this was done and agreed. And as I said there is the fourteen-day cool-off period / that – .

THREE You said.

TWO *holds up the pen.*

TWO Can I ask you to – ?

Beat.

All this-these paragraphs here are just making sure you understand the process and that you agree that you came to this decision without any undue influence from any official – and that –

THREE that?

TWO There, that

THREE right

TWO *that* is just stating that you are of sound mind – did you bring the documentation from your GP to –

THREE I have them, originals not copies –

TWO good. The rest of it is pretty much about us countersigning and agreeing who was in the room and at what time you gave us the decision and that you are of sound mind and all / that.

THREE And the other three / pages?

TWO   That, pretty much doesn't – nothing that reflects or affects you, mainly for our office purposes, do take your time and take the time to read, I wouldn't want you to sign if you weren't sure –

THREE   I am / sure.

TWO   weren't sure what you were signing for I meant.

THREE starts to read the documents in detail.
Beat.
Beat.

Most people do find them pretty straightforward and just... sign.

THREE continues to read. It takes a while.
ONE and TWO become increasingly self-conscious.
Beat.
As THREE holds the paperwork the shake in her hand is more apparent.
Beat.

Eventually she takes the pen. It shakes in her hand.

THREE   Here?

TWO   No nope – sorry, no. Just there, under there. And if you could write clearly in capitals your decision – there – and to sign under it there. Then it would be just to date it to the side –

THREE   you've got the stamp.

TWO   As well as the stamp. The stamp shows we know the date, you dating it shows you agree.

THREE hesitates.

THREE   What is the date today?

ONE	Twelfth.
	THREE *attempts to sign. The pen trembles in her hand, it is difficult for her. She restarts a number of times.*
TWO	(*quietly*) I can get more copies if I need to.
	THREE *becomes slightly self-conscious but is determined to get it done. The writing is awful, the process frustrating and a little humiliating.*
	THREE *signs, copy after copy, painstakingly slowly.*
	And one more... just... (there). Yeh. Thanks. That's... that's almost – .
	TWO *noisily and heavy-handedly stamps the date on all copies.*
	Love this bit.
THREE	You read the letter.
	TWO *shoots an uncertain look to* ONE.
	Any surprises?
TWO	...Depends on what you're expecting.
THREE	I expect nothing.
TWO	...I need to take these back to –
ONE	leave them there.
	TWO *stays reluctantly.*
THREE	(*quietly*)...Fuck.
	Beat.
ONE	You don't have to read it.
THREE	I know I don't.
ONE	You don't have / to –

THREE   I know I don't you don't have to tell me
         I don't.

ONE   Don't read it. Don't read it.

TWO   …Y'know I'm not bein bad but you-you
         could take a copy home if that would help –

ONE   take a copy – we have to retain the original –
         but you could take a copy home and have
         someone there read it for you, to / you.

THREE   And who would that be then? My kids? My
         husband? Suzette or my friends who I don't
         now have?

ONE

THREE   You want me to take that thing that he's
         written – written on into where we live, where
         we are, where my kids are – that thing that
         he's written with his, tone. His intonations.
         His accent. His breath, weight of his breath.
         His spit. His smell. His odour, his sweat, the
         weight of his sweat, his…

         Them fuckin blue blue eyes, his eyes in my…
         and it will be in his voice that I hear, that I
         hear it in that I read it, that I read it in,
         because *you* wouldn't read it – no. No.

ONE   I'm / sorry –

THREE   Do not utter that you're 'sorry'. *Do not*.

ONE   No.

TWO   There's no obligation for you to / read it.

ONE   He doesn't know either way, won't know
         either / way.

TWO   We have to tell him it's been received by us
         that's the only thing –

ONE   the only requirement –

TWO	on our part.
THREE	I don't trust what-the-fuck you'd say to him. Maybe you'd treat him a bit better that you treatin / me.
ONE	That's not fair –
THREE	I think it is.

THREE *eyes the envelope.*
Beat.

A weariness about her.
Beat.
Beat.

(*quietly*)…Open it for me.

ONE	What? I didn't quite –
THREE	would you open it for me.
ONE	If you're sure –
THREE	I'm not sure.

ONE *carefully opens the envelope.*

TWO	It's not in the original envelope or anything we – once it's passed through our system we always rehouse it.
THREE	'Rehouse'?
ONE	Re-envelope.
TWO	Stops people, I think the first thing people do is, sniff it or, try to get some sort of residue of a memory of…
THREE	
TWO	No I don't get it but…
THREE	

TWO   And also, y'know – .

THREE

TWO   A hygiene thing. Y'know.

THREE

*ONE isn't sure what to do with the opened
envelope that contains the letter.*

ONE   D'you want me to...?

*THREE watches the envelope.
They watch THREE.*

Beat.

*THREE goes to say something, doesn't. She
makes a tiny gesture for it. ONE carefully
hands it over to her.*

*THREE watches it with difficulty, suspicious
of it and of her own reactions.*

TWO   D'you want us to leave?

THREE   *(quietly)...* Yes.

Beat.

ONE and TWO leave the room.

*THREE carefully pulls the folded letter from
the envelope. The shake in her hand self-
consciously visible.*

She carefully unfolds the letter.

*She notices the writing on only one side of A4.
The letter is not long.*

THREE starts to read the handwritten letter.

Her hand still carries a tremble.

Beat.
Beat.

It is an effort.

Beat.

She reads.
It is taking it out of her. The tremble in her hand increases slightly.
She continues to read.

Beat.

End.

www.nickhernbooks.co.uk

facebook.com/nickhernbooks

twitter.com/nickhernbooks